Whispered Longings

An Anthology of Poems on Love's Silent Longing

<u>Copyright</u>

Dedication

"To the muse who ignited the flame,
Whose presence inspired every line,
Though our paths diverged, love remains,
In whispered words, our hearts entwine."

Contents

Inroduction

"Whispered Longings" is a heartfelt compilation of poems that deeply explore the emotional and often heart-wrenching realm of unreturned love. This anthology is inspired by personal encounters with yearning, quiet adoration, and the longing for a love that remains unspoken or unreciprocated. Through a mix of poetic styles and forms, these poems unravel the delicate emotions that come with one-sided love, capturing both the sweet moments of connection and the pain of unfulfilled desires.

The verses in this collection embody the spirit of love's silent longing, interweaving themes of friendship, devotion, and the challenge of moving on from a love that was never meant to be. Each poem tells its own unique story, encouraging you, the reader, to reflect on the fine line between love and friendship, and the courage it takes to reveal your true feelings.

This anthology also highlights the beauty of unvoiced emotions and the potency of silence, skillfully blending evocative imagery with sincere expressions of love that go beyond spoken words. As you delve into these lines, you'll discover the determination and resilience of those who have loved from a distance, and perhaps find solace in knowing that others have shared your experience of unrequited love.

My sincerest hope is that "Whispered Longings" connects with those who have experienced the bittersweet feeling of loving someone deeply without the promise of their love in return. May these poems provide comfort and understanding, and serve as a gentle reminder that even in the face of unrequited love, our hearts continue to seek connection, hope, and the magical power of love

<u>*In the Field of Sorrow*</u>

In a field of sorrow I lay,
Tears of pain I cannot sway
My heart is broken , my soul is bare
I wish for love, but no one is there

I search for hope in this world of woe
But all I find is emptiness and blows
I cry out for someone to hear
But only silence greets my ears

In this dark and lovely night
I hold on to what little light
But even that begins to fade
As the pain and sorrow invade

I long for the touch of a loving hand
To heal the wounds and make me stand
But alas, I am all alone
In this never-ending heartache and moan

So I lay here, in this field of despair
Praying for a love beyond compare
But untill that day may come
I am trapped in this sorrow, forever numb

<u>The Sculptor's Masterpiece</u>

With chisel in hand, I carve my love
The marble whispers secrets from above
A masterpiece revealed, as passions prove

Each stroke reveals the truth beneath the stone
The beauty of a love that's yet unknown
With chisel in hand, I carve my love

A heart that beats, a touch that's gently sown
As tender as the love that I have shown
A masterpiece revealed, as passions prove

A sculpture standing tall, emotions grown
In hidden depths, our love remains unshown
With chisel in hand, I carve my love

Yet deep within the marble's cold embrace
Our love's eternal fire finds its place
A masterpiece revealed, as passions prove

And as I sculpt, our love's embrace I'll trace
In every line, our story interlaced
With chisel in hand, I carve my love
A masterpiece revealed, as passions prove

The Phantom Waltz

In moonlit dreams, we danced beneath the stars,
A phantom waltz, two souls entwined as one.
With every step, we traced our love's memoirs,
Yet still, your touch, like morning mist, was gone.

I longed to feel the warmth of your embrace,
To lose myself within your tender gaze.
But shadows lingered, cold and out of place,
My heart, a captive of love's endless maze.

A ghostly partner, always out of reach,
The whispered promise of a love so rare.
In every dream, I tried to breach
The distance, but you vanished in thin air.

And so, I wake, and face the dawn alone,
Accepting that our dance will ne'er be known.

<u>*The Barista's Blend*</u>

Steam rises,
As beans are ground,
Barista's love,
Infused in each cup,
Served without sound.

The perfect blend,
Bitter and sweet,
Love unspoken,
In aromatic notes,
Her heart skips a beat.

Cocoa and spice,
The flavors swirl,
In coffee's depths,
Their unrequited love,
A hidden pearl.

Each morning,
She crafts her brew,
Pouring her heart,
Into every cup,
Hoping he knew.

A silent toast,
To love's embrace,
As he savors,
The subtle warmth,
Of her secret grace.

<u>The Birdwatcher's Song</u>

Among the trees, the birds sing their songs,
Each melody a balm for the heart,
Unrequited love echoes along.

He listens close, a part of nature's art,
In avian choruses, he finds,
A tender solace, as the day departs.

The robin's trill, a reminder of times,
When fleeting glances led to sweet smiles,
Love's language, spoken without reason or rhyme.

The sparrow's tune, a gentle lullaby,
Whispering hope for love to return,
A song that carries through the sky.

With every note, the birdwatcher learns,
To find beauty in unspoken love,
In the melodies that his heart yearns.

And as the sun sets, the songs above,
Merge into a symphony of grace,
A testament to unrequited love.

<u>Silent Serenade</u>

In twilight's hush, I strummed my heart's lament,
A silent serenade, my love for you.
Each note, a whispered plea, a soft intent,
To sing the words my lips could never do.

From tender strings, my love took flight,
A melody, a secret symphony.
With bated breath, I hoped it might
Someday reach your ears and set me free.

Through night's embrace, the music soared,
A gentle breeze to carry it along.
And though the chance seemed slim, I still implored,
That you might hear and know my love's sweet song.

In silent serenades, my love abides,
A hopeful anthem, where my heart resides.

<u>*Letters Unsent*</u>

In ink and paper, secrets softly bled,
A thousand letters, words I dare not say.
To your embrace, my longing heart misled.

Each page, a testament to love unsaid,
Emotions raw, yet hidden far away.
In ink and paper, secrets softly bled.

I wrote of dreams, of love's eternal thread,
My pen revealing all I wished to convey.
To your embrace, my longing heart misled.

Unspoken words, their power still undread,
These letters, tucked away in disarray.
In ink and paper, secrets softly bled.

The courage to confess, forever fled,
But still, these letters, night and day I weigh.
To your embrace, my longing heart misled.

A silent solace, where my thoughts are led,
Unsent, these letters keep my hope at bay.
In ink and paper, secrets softly bled,
To your embrace, my longing heart misled.

The Dance of Shadows

In the twilight of my longing,
We danced the dance of shadows,
Silent steps, unspoken love,
A waltz only we could follow.

A love that could not be contained,
Yet never stepped into the light,
We moved in sync, but far apart,
Bound by the chains of the night.

The music played, a haunting tune,
Our hearts entwined, but never true,
For though we danced in harmony,
Our love was something we could not choose.

And so, we bowed and walked away,
Our shadows fading with the sun,
As we embraced a life apart,
Our dance of shadows left undone.

But in the twilight of my memory,
I find solace in the past,
For the dance of shadows taught me love,
Can be both beautiful and vast.

<u>Echoes in the Hallway</u>

Footsteps echo, soft,
Whispers of the love we lost,
Silent memories.

In shadows, I dwell,
Holding on to fleeting dreams,
Heartache's quiet dance.

Time drifts, seasons change,
Yet echoes of love remain,
Persistent and true.

Unrequited love,
An endless maze, I traverse,
Searching for an end.

Embrace solitude,
Aching heart finds its own strength,
Resilient soul heals.

Echoes fade to hush,
Love's memory lingers still,
Gently I move on.

<u>The Ghost of You</u>

In the quiet corners of my heart,
A ghost of you resides,
Lingering in the shadows,
Of dreams unspoken and denied.

A whisper of a longing,
The echo of your name,
A silent song we danced to,
In a world we never claimed.

How do I chase your specter,
From the chambers of my soul?
How do I release the phantom grip,
That keeps my heart on hold?

Yet I know, dear apparition,
That our love could never be,
For it was built on fragile whispers,
In the realm of fantasy.

As I step into the sunlight,
And leave your ghost behind,
I'll treasure the sweet memories,
Of a love we never defined.

In time, the ache will vanish,
As your shadow fades away,
But the strength I gained in letting go,
Will forever in me stay.

<u>*Uncharted Waters*</u>

In uncharted waters, my ship set sail,
With dreams of you in every gale,
A journey I took, unspoken and blind,
In search of a love I'd never find.

I traveled far across the sea,
A lighthouse in your eyes I'd see,
But stormy waves and treacherous tides,
Would keep me from your loving side.

My compass spun, direction lost,
I paid for love at the highest cost,
But as the tempest began to clear,
The truth of my heartache would appear.

I turned my ship toward the shore,
My longing heart could take no more,
I sought solace on solid ground,
Where a new love could be found.

In time, my wounds began to heal,
As I let go of love not real,
I learned to navigate life's seas,
With newfound strength and clarity.

I'll always cherish the love I sought,
In the uncharted waters where I was caught,
For it taught me to be brave and strong,
And to find my way when things go wrong.

The Siren's Lament

In the deepest depths of the ocean blue,
A siren sang a mournful tune,
Her voice filled with a love so true,
Yet destined to be met with ruin.

Her heart belonged to a sailor bold,
Whose ship she'd seen from her watery home,
But he knew her not, his heart untold,
As he sailed the seas, forever to roam.

Each night she'd sing her love to him,
Her voice carried on the waves,
But her song was lost to the winds,
Her love, a secret locked away.

One night, the sea grew dark and cold,
As storm clouds filled the sky,
The siren knew her love untold,
Could no longer be denied.

She sang a final, haunting song,
Her heartache in every note,
As she let go of love forlorn,
And set her sorrow afloat.

As her lament filled the ocean wide,
A newfound strength began to rise,
For in the depths of her heartache,
The siren learned to find her light.

<u>**The Gaze Unmet**</u>

In the crowded room, my eyes sought thine,
A connection, a spark, a fleeting chance.
But as the stars align, our paths collide,
The gaze unmet, my heart's desire veiled.
I wondered if your eyes would ever see,
The longing in my own, a love revealed.

In solitude, I dreamed of love revealed,
As tender whispers carried thoughts of thine.
In moonlit dreams, I hoped that you would see,
That fate would grant our hearts a second chance.
Yet every time we met, my love remained veiled,
Invisible, as fate refused to collide.

And in my dreams, our separate worlds collide,
A sweet collision, where my love's revealed.
But waking hours show a truth still veiled,
A quiet yearning in my soul for thine.
I pray the universe grants me a chance,
To let you know, to let your heart truly see.

I watched you from afar, your eyes to see,
Your laughter, your smile, as our worlds collide.
Each fleeting moment, I sought for a chance,
To speak the words, my aching heart revealed.
But every time, my courage failed with thine,
A whispered truth, forevermore veiled.

In shadows, I remained, my face half-veiled,
My heart a secret, no one else could see.
A quiet hope, my love would reach to thine,
Two parallel paths, destined not to collide.
And still, I held on to a love revealed,
Each whispered wish, a hope for one more chance.

A final plea, a desperate, yearning chance,
To break the chains, and leave my love unveiled.
To show the world the truth, my heart revealed,
And let you see the love I held within.
To make our lives, our stories, finally collide,
To intertwine my longing heart with thine.

In dreams, I sought a chance, your eyes to see,
But love, veiled and hidden, refused to collide.
My heart revealed, still longs for love from thine.

<u>The Unpicked Rose</u>

A rose left unpicked,
In the garden of my heart,
Yearns for your sweet touch,
To be cherished and adored,
Love's potential left untold.

Petals soft and red,
Longing for your tender gaze,
A love unspoken,
Silent beauty lost in time,
The rose withers, untended.

Unrequited love,
Like the rose, a fragile bloom,
Touched by morning frost,
Waiting for the sun to shine,
And thaw its frozen petals.

In the garden's shade,
The rose learns to stand alone,
Roots deep and steadfast,
Unpicked, yet with strength to grow,
Love transformed, a rose reborn.

The unpicked rose thrives,
A symbol of resilience,
Beauty undiminished,
Though unclaimed by your sweet hand,
A testament to love's strength.

In the fading light,
The rose finds solace and peace,
Embracing its fate,
Unrequited love endures,
Yet stronger in its own right.

<u>The Unsent Message</u>

Within the glowing screen, my love confessed,
A message typed, but never sent, I stressed.

In digital embrace, my feelings rest,
Unsent, my heart's desires remain suppressed.

With trembling hands, I typed what I professed,
Yet fear held back the words, and I transgressed.

The cursor blinks, as if to second-guess,
A message waiting, love remains unexpressed.

My heart's turmoil, in silence, I redressed,
The unsent message hidden, uncaressed.

In quiet strength, I learn to coalesce,
A message unsent, love undressed, I progress.

The Untraveled Bridge

Upon the edge of love's untraveled bridge,
I stood and gazed upon the other side,
A distant shore, beyond my reach and ridge.

With tender hope, I yearned to cross and glide,
To touch the heart that seemed forever far,
Yet, fear and doubt kept me from love's sweet tide.

I gazed upon the moon, the sun, the stars,
And wondered if my love could ever span,
The daunting chasm, love's unfathomed scars.

With every step, I longed to understand,
The path that led to your embracing heart,
But destiny, it seemed, had other plans.

At last, I turned, accepting we're apart,
A stronger soul, I left love's bridge unmarred.

The Silent Storm

Swaying in the wind, my love concealed,
The whispers of my heart, a quiet plea.
Overhead, the clouds of doubt congealed,
Reflecting all the pain that dwells in me.
My love, a silent storm, a breathless sea.

Yearning for a touch, an echoed glance,
Eager to be heard, to take a chance.
Aching for your warmth, our hearts to dance,
Resilient, I weather love's hard stance.

In shadows, I embrace a quiet strength,
Lulled by the storm's song, a whispered hymn.
Evolving, healing, growing in length,
No longer held by love's unyielding whim.

The silent storm, a testament of grace,
Shifting with the winds, my heart retraced.
Overcoming fear, I find my place,
Reborn, I stand with love's newfound embrace,
My heart, now calm, has weathered the storm's chase.

<u>*The Astronomer's Star*</u>

In cosmic dance, I see our love afar,
My heart, an astronomer, seeking light,
I trace your name upon a distant star.

I search the skies to find where you now are,
A beacon shining through the endless night,
In cosmic dance, I see our love afar.

Each constellation, a map of memoirs,
A tapestry of memories, burning bright,
I trace your name upon a distant star.

My telescope, a portal to your heart,
Revealing love's elusive, secret sight,
In cosmic dance, I see our love afar.

Though galaxies and worlds may keep us apart,
I find solace in the stars' guiding light,
I trace your name upon a distant star.

And as the heavens turn, a cosmic bazaar,
Our love endures, unyielding in its fight,
In cosmic dance, I see our love afar,
I trace your name upon a distant star.

Autumn's Embrace

In the autumn of my heart,
I loved you like a falling leaf,
Drifting on a gentle breeze,
Bound for ground and destined grief.

Our love, a transient display,
Of colors vibrant, yet brief,
A symphony of warmth and gold,
In the chill of life's belief.

I yearned to hold you close to me,
But like the leaves, you slipped away,
Caught in the winds of circumstance,
A love unspoken, couldn't stay.

As the cold of winter settled in,
I learned to let my love depart,
For in the barren trees and frost,
I found the strength to heal my heart.

35

In time, the seasons turned again,
And spring brought love anew,
But the lessons from my autumn love,
Will remain, forever true

The Ocean's Embrace

The ocean's waves embrace my longing heart,
As I release my love into the sea,
A whispered wish, for us to never part,
The ocean's waves embrace my longing heart.
Yet destiny has torn our souls apart,
My love, like driftwood, lost in the debris.
The ocean's waves embrace my longing heart,
As I release my love into the sea.

With every ebb and flow, my love remains,
A testament to passion's endless tide,
In every crest, I hear your voice, refrains,
A serenade, forever by my side.

The Distant Shore

From the distant shore, I gazed,
Across the ocean of my heart,
To where your love resided,
A world that kept us apart.

The waves carried my dreams,
My wishes upon the sea,
To reach you in the distance,
Where our love could never be.

But in the ebb and flow of tides,
I found the strength to sail,
To navigate the ocean of my heart,
With love as my guiding gale.

Though our love was but a dream,
On the distant shore, I'll stand,
With newfound courage and hope,
On the horizon, a love so grand.

<u>The Moonlit Sonata</u>

Underneath the moonlit sky,
I'd play a sonata for you and I,
A haunting melody of love untold,
In every note, my heart unfolds.

The keys, they whispered of my desire,
A secret love, a burning fire,
But you could never hear my song,
For you were not where you belonged.

My love, a symphony in the dark,
A moonlit sonata, a hidden spark,
A tune that only I could play,
While the world remained at bay.

But as the night turned into day,
I knew I had to walk away,
To let the music fade to silence,
And embrace a love without pretense.

The moonlit sonata, a memory,
A testament to love's sweet folly,
Though our love was never meant to be,
It taught me how to set my heart free

<u>The Unspoken Overture</u>

In friendship's notes, a symphony we played
Our laughter's rhythm, syncopated grace
But deep within, a hidden melody
A song of love, composed yet unperformed

With every chord, my heartstrings resonated
A secret tune, an aria in vain
Yet even as I yearned to share my heart
My voice was silenced by the fear of loss

In quiet moments, our song's memory
Still echoes softly, a tender serenade
The notes of love, a dance upon the page
An unplayed symphony of whispered dreams

Though time has passed and we have moved apart
The music lingers, an unfinished score

In sleep, I dream of all we could have been
A duet of love, harmonious embrace
But then I wake to find the truth remains
An unrequited love, a silent phrase

Yet still I cherish every note we shared
Our friendship's song, a treasured masterpiece
And though unplayed, my symphony of love
Will always hold a place within my heart

<u>*Love's Labyrinth*</u>

Within the maze, I wander every turn,
Each twist and bend reflecting my desire,
A labyrinth of love I must discern,
To find the center, where my heart aspires.
The hedges high, as if to mock my yearning,
A challenge to my soul, love's path to learn.

I dare to tread, compelled to seek and learn,
My heart, a compass guiding every turn,
Each step brings forth a new and fervent yearning,
A passion born from deep and ardent desire.
Through the labyrinth, I chase what I aspire,
Unraveling love's mystery, I sojourn.

Through twists and turns, I navigate my sojourn,
In pursuit of love, its lessons I shall learn,
My quest unyielding, seeking to aspire,
A way through the maze, with each careful turn.
In shadows deep, I find my heart's desire,
The labyrinth's core, where love's flame is burning.

My spirit ignites, fueled by love's burning,
A beacon in the darkness of my sojourn,
The fire guides me, illuminating desire,
A light that teaches me the way to learn,
To navigate the labyrinth's every turn,
My heart and mind aligned, they both aspire.

To the center, where my dreams do aspire,
I journey forth, love's labyrinth still burning,
Each footstep leads me closer with each turn,
A map of love unfolding on this sojourn,
The walls, once barriers, now help me learn,
To follow the path that leads to my desire.

And in the end, I find my true desire,
The heart's goal, to which I longed to aspire,
A labyrinth's gift, the wisdom that I learn,
A testament to love's eternal burning,
No longer lost within this endless sojourn,
I've mastered the maze, and life's fateful turns.

From each turn, I've grown, and love's desire
Has led me to aspire, on this sojourn,
To learn from the labyrinth, love's flame burning.

Unspoken Symphony

In my heart, a song
Unplayed, a symphony waits
Love's notes yet unheard

The melody of longing
Yearns for the perfect moment

Strings sing of our love
In tender harmonies, soft
Aching to be shared

The unspoken symphony
A secret crescendo builds

One day, love's music
Shall break free, and serenade
The world with our tale

Unrequited love transformed
Into a symphony heard

The Dreamer's Flight

In dreams, we soar through boundless, azure skies

Our hands entwined, hearts beating in tandem

We glide, ascending to love's paradise

A fleeting moment of sweet abandon

I whisper words unsaid, soft confessions

But morning sun disrupts the fantasy

Awakening to face reality

Unspoken love and silent affection

The dreamer's flight to love remains grounded

The Sculptor's Longing

In chiseled stone, my love for you appears,
A silent plea, carved deep within the art.
I sculpt your form, in hope to quell my fears,
Yet marble's cold, a mimic of your heart.
A masterwork of love, I stand apart,
A sculptor's longing, etched in time and tears.

With every strike, I craft your face so dear,
Your eyes, your lips, the essence of your soul.
But in my heart, a truth remains severe,
The lifeless stone can never make me whole.
And as I toil, my love it perseveres,
A sculptor's longing, etched in time and tears.

In silent nights, my dreams are filled with you,
Your laughter, and your gentle, tender touch.
Awake, I find solace in my work, it's true,
Yet stone can't quench the fire that burns as much.
A sculptor's longing, etched in time and tears,
In chiseled stone, my love for you appears.

The Poet's Quill

My quill,
It writes the words,
My heart cannot convey,
A testament of unspoken love,
In ink.

Each line,
A secret wish,
A dream I dare not share,
The poet's quill reveals my truth,
In verse.

I pen,
My longing soul,
In hopes that you might read,
The depth of love that lies beneath,
My words.

Verses,
Like autumn leaves,
Dance softly in the breeze,
Their hidden meanings waiting to,
Be found.

One day,
Perhaps you'll know,
My love was always there,
Hidden within the poet's lines,
Unsaid.

And still,
The poet's quill,
Continues to inscribe,
Enduring love, a testament,
In ink.

<u>*The Gardener's Seed*</u>

A seed of love, I plant in secret soil,
In hopes that it may one day bloom and grow,
Yet hidden deep, my love remains in toil,
A gardener's heart, concealed in shadows' throw.

I tend the seed with care, through day and night,
A seed of love, I plant in secret soil,
My heart, the gardener, dreams of love's delight,
But fate, it seems, has other plans to foil.

In quiet patience, I await the day,
When love's sweet flower might finally show,
A seed of love, I plant in secret soil,
And pray that it may flourish, strong and whole.

Though unrequited love remains concealed,
A gardener's love, in time, may yet be healed.

The Painter's Muse

In colors bright, I paint your face divine,
A masterpiece, my heart's unspoken muse.
My love for you, I cannot quite define,
Each brushstroke, a confession I refuse.

A masterpiece, my heart's unspoken muse,
I pour my soul into each vibrant hue.
Each brushstroke, a confession I refuse,
Yet, on the canvas, my love shines through.

I pour my soul into each vibrant hue,
A portrait of a love that can't be mine.
Yet, on the canvas, my love shines through,
My longing heart in colors intertwined.

A portrait of a love that can't be mine,
My love for you, I cannot quite define.
My longing heart in colors intertwined,
In colors bright, I paint your face divine.

<u>The Alchemist's Desire</u>

Within the ancient chambers, shadows dance
An alchemist, I toil through the night
To transform my love, I take a chance
With fire and metal, secrets brought to light
The crucible, a vessel for my heart
I seek to change the nature of desire
To bend and mold the truth that I require
But love's elusive essence slips away

The alchemy of passion I explore
As gold from lead, I hope to conjure more
But in the end, the truth is plain to see
Love's nature can't be altered, forced, or swayed
In quiet stillness, I begin to learn
The love I yearn for cannot be remade

With humble heart, I cease the fiery churn
The alchemist must face what he has spurned
For love's transformation is not earned
But found within the heart's pure honesty
In quiet stillness, I begin to learn
The love I yearn for cannot be remade

<u>*A Love Unraveled*</u>

We walked along the shores of memory
Our laughter intertwined with ocean's song
A tapestry of love, a reverie
Yet in your eyes, the spark did not belong

I still recall the warmth of your embrace
A fleeting touch, the brush of fingertips
A moment's peace within this tender space
But on my lips, the taste of love still slips

And in the autumn air, we shared our dreams
Our breaths entwined in wisps of silver mist
Yet as the sun dipped low, my heart did scream
For in your gaze, love's fire did not persist

Through every tender moment, bittersweet
A love unraveled, but never complete
Now, as I trace the echoes of our past
In memory's hold, our love forever lasts

<u>The Conductor's Symphony</u>

Baton raised,
The Conductor guides,
Love's silent symphony,
Unrequited strains, yet yearning,
Unheard.

Crescendo,
Emotions soar high,
Heartstrings compose the score,
In the melody, love's bittersweet,
Release.

Harmony,
Resonates with pain,
Each note, a tender plea,
Love's unspoken song, hopeful for,
Requiem.

Pianissimo,
Soft, yet persistent,
Love's symphony whispers,
Delicate strains, weaving through,
Silence.

Vivace,
Life's tempo quickens,
Love's song echoes within,
Unfaltering, strong, despite the,
Distance.

Finale,
Symphony's end nears,
A bittersweet farewell,
The Conductor lowers the baton,
Love's close.

<u>Love's Fading Echo</u>

As silent whispers on a moonlit night,
The echoes of our love begin to fade,
I stand alone, embraced by twilight's light,
A somber elegy for love unmade.

Once vibrant, like the colors of the dawn,
The memories of you now dulled by time,
Through quiet forests, I now tread forlorn,
The path ahead uncertain, yet I climb.

For in my heart, a tender flame still burns,
A flickering reminder of our past,
But like the leaves in autumn, love now turns,
And I must face the truth, it could not last.

With every step, love's echoes grow more faint,
Yet in my soul, your memory remains a saint.

<u>*The Glassblower's Flame*</u>

A glassblower's flame, it shapes my heart
In molten hues of red and gold desire
Through fire and air, love's fragile art

I breathe the life, a dance of heat and fire
The passion burns, my soul it molds and bends
In molten hues of red and gold desire

This craft of love, to shape, to sculpt, to mend
My hands, they tremble, knowing love's sweet pain
The passion burns, my soul it molds and bends

For love, like glass, is delicate and strained
One touch too firm, and all would shatter, break
My hands, they tremble, knowing love's sweet pain

Yet in this fragility, beauty wakes
A love that's formed, both radiant and bright
One touch too firm, and all would shatter, break

The glassblower's flame, it shapes my heart
A love that's formed, both radiant and bright
Through fire and air, love's fragile art

The Shadow's Dance

In twilight's realm, I watch the shadows dance,
As silhouettes entwined with dark desires,
My love for you, an ever-shifting trance,
A ghostly waltz that flickers and expires.

I reach for you, but find just empty air,
A phantom touch, a longing unfulfilled,
For in the shadows, love is fleeting, rare,
A whispered dream that's never truly stilled.

Yet still I chase the shadow's fleeting grace,
In moonlit glades and sunlit forest glens,
In hopes that I might glimpse your tender face,
And hold you close, if only for a moment's span.

But shadows dance and twist, forever out of reach,
My love, a fleeting specter, evermore to teach.

A Love Undimmed

As shadows fall and darkness starts to creep,
And sorrow weighs upon my weary soul,
I find my strength, a love that runs so deep,
A beacon shining bright, a love undimmed.

Through stormy nights and days of endless rain,
Unspoken words and tears that freely flow,
I hold to hope that one day you'll know,
A beacon shining bright, a love undimmed.

For in the vast expanse of night's embrace,
My heart, a lighthouse guiding through despair,
Its beam unwavering, steady in its place,
A beacon shining bright, a love undimmed.

The Chocolatier's Sweet

A chocolatier with love bittersweet
Crafted a treat, a heart's delight to meet
He poured in his soul, his hopes, and desires
And wrapped it in gold, as love's flame aspires
But the sweet remained his, a love incomplete

<u>*The Unseen Artist*</u>

I painted you with colors unseen,
In a portrait of love's tender dream,
Each stroke a wish, a hope, a plea,
For a love that could never be.

My palette filled with shades of yearning,
I crafted a world, our love's own haven,
But the canvas remained untouched by you,
For you were blind to love's hidden hue.

In the shadows, I watched you walk away,
My masterpiece unseen, my heart in disarray,
I knew I had to let you go,
For our love was hidden, a world unknown.

As I stepped back from the canvas grand,
I learned to paint with a different hand,
To create a world of love and light,
That would no longer be kept from sight.

The unseen artist, I am no more,
My love unchained, my heart restored,
For in the colors of my broken heart,
I found the strength to make a new start.

The Astronomer's Cosmos

Amidst the vast expanse, a comet's trail
Reflects the ardor of my longing heart
It streaks across the sky, a silent wail

In every meteor shower's graceful arc
I see the fragile beauty of our love
A fleeting glimpse, yet etched upon the dark

A black hole's pull, impossible to shove
It draws me in, unyielding, ever strong
My love for you, a force I cannot prove

Yet as the cosmos whispers love's sweet song
The galaxies align, and in their thrall
I find the strength to carry ever on

Within the boundless universe I call
Your name, my love, unrequited, yet enthralled

<u>The Calligrapher's Verse</u>

With ink and quill, I write my heart's desire,
Elegant strokes revealing love unspoken.
Upon the parchment, words and feelings intertwine,
Graceful lines bearing witness to my longing,
Each verse a testament to the truth of love's nature,
My pen a conduit for unrequited dreams.

In dreams, I see your face, the object of my desire,
But upon waking, reality's weight, unspoken.
Love's truth lies buried within my soul's nature,
Yet I write, seeking solace in this endless longing,
Our story told in ink, our lives forever intertwine,
My heart's yearning spelled out in delicate dreams.

Dreams of you haunt my every waking moment,
Yet in the silent corners of the night, desire
Burns, as our destinies twist and intertwine.
My love for you remains silent, unspoken,
A secret held close, an eternal longing,
Inscribed in the very essence of my nature.

For it is in my nature to love, to yearn,
To reach for the stars, to chase elusive dreams.
Though I know the bitter sting of longing,
I cannot quell the fire of my desire.
I find solace in these verses, unspoken,
My love for you, eternal, will forever intertwine.

With every stroke, our fates, they intertwine,
My love for you, an intrinsic part of my nature,
In the quiet recesses of my heart, unspoken.
Yet, I find solace in the art of my dreams,
The eloquence of my pen, the solace of my desire,
My quill, a balm to soothe my aching longing.

And in these words, I find a refuge for my longing,
A sanctuary where our lives can intertwine,
Where I can pour out the depths of my desire,
Revealing the essence of my truest nature,
In the quiet corners of the night, I chase my dreams,
Hoping that one day, love will no longer be unspoken.

No longer unspoken, my longing finds a voice,
Our destinies intertwine, immortalized in dreams,
Love's nature revealed, an enduring testament of desire.

The Photographer's Memory

Fleeting moments caught
In a frozen frame of time
Love's memory stays

Unrequited love's
Soft glow, captured in shadows
And light's tender dance

In each photograph
A story untold, yet shared
Eyes meet, hearts whisper

Cherished memories
Locked within a silver box
Forever treasured

Through the lens, I see
A world where love can flourish
In silence, it speaks

Time's passage observed
In these photos of our past
Still, my love endures

The Librarian's Whisper

Librarian's hush
Whispers
Unspoken love blooms
Pages rustle softly
Secrets

Books hold
Emotions
Tales of yearning hearts
Between lines, a lover's sigh
Hidden

Love's words
Caressed by
Fingers tracing prose
In quiet moments, feelings found
Unsaid

Volumes
Surround us
Knowledge held within
Yet love's truth remains elusive
Silent

Endless
Aisles of books
Sheltering hearts and minds
In their embrace, I find solace
Unseen

Potter's Creation

With hands submerged in Earth's embrace, I find
The clay beneath my fingers takes the form
Of love unspoken, ever on my mind
And in my heart, a quiet storm

This vessel of my love, I shape with care
Each curve a testament to longing's plight
The fire, it burns, our secret laid bare
Yet in the shadows, hidden from sight

In kiln's embrace, the fragile clay withstands
The heat and pressure, stronger it becomes
Just as my love, within life's shifting sands
Holds fast, unwavering, my heart succumbs

My masterpiece complete, I stand in awe
This vessel, love unspoken, without flaw

<u>The Lighthouse Keeper's Beacon</u>

The lighthouse keeper tends a guiding light,
A beacon shining through the darkest storm,
In lonely nights, he dreams of love's delight,
He tends the flames, to keep his spirit warm.

A beacon shining through the darkest storm,
His love, unrequited, yet burning bright,
He tends the flames, to keep his spirit warm,
The lighthouse stands, a symbol of his fight.

His love, unrequited, yet burning bright,
He sends his light across the churning sea,
The lighthouse stands, a symbol of his fight,
In waves of longing, love's vast mystery.

He sends his light across the churning sea,
In lonely nights, he dreams of love's delight,
In waves of longing, love's vast mystery,
The lighthouse keeper tends a guiding light.

<u>The Storyteller's Tale</u>

A storyteller weaves a tale of love,
A tale of unrequited dreams and tears,
A tale of hope, that soars like wings of doves,
A tale that echoes through the distant years.

In whispered words, he shares the memories,
The stolen glances, laughter in the breeze,
He tells of secret wishes, reveries,
Of love that blooms and fades like autumn leaves.

And as he speaks, a bittersweet refrain,
The listeners find solace in his voice,
For in each heart, there lies a similar pain,
A love unspoken, made by fate's own choice.

The tale concludes, a quiet sigh is heard,
The storyteller's love, immortalized in word.

<u>The Glassmaker's Shard</u>

Upon the glowing furnace, love takes form,
The glassmaker, with skillful hands, gives life,
To fragile beauty, born within the storm,
Of passion, longing, heartache, and of strife.

A delicate shard, his love's embodiment,
Reflects the fire's dance within its core,
Yet, with a touch, the glass may crack or dent,
A love unspoken, shatters on the floor.

This fragile shard, a testament to pain,
The glassmaker, with tears, accepts his fate,
For every shard that shatters, love remains,
A memory, bittersweet, and innate.

And thus, the glassmaker, with hands so skilled,
Embraces love, unbroken, unfulfilled.

A Love Unseen

In the depth of night, I whispered
To the moon of a love unseen,
A tale of longing and desire,
For you, my heart's sweet dream.

The moon, a silent witness,
Bathed in silver, cool and bright,
Held my secrets and my heartaches,
For a love that never took flight.

Yet, in the darkness, I found solace,
The night sky, my confidante,
And as the dawn broke, I discovered,
The strength to love and to want.

For though our love never flourished,
And remained hidden in the night,
I'll cherish the memories and moonbeams,
And emerge stronger in the light.

<u>The Weaver's Tapestry</u>

I weave my love into a tapestry,
A tapestry of dreams and secret sighs,
In every thread, a hint of you and me,
A silent longing, hidden from your eyes.

Each color tells a story of its own,
A memory of moments shared and gone,
Yet as I weave, my heart begins to moan,
For unrequited love remains alone.

The tapestry, a masterpiece of time,
Intricate with patterns, rich in hue,
My love, a secret woven in each line,
The weaver's art, a tribute to love's due.

In every thread, my longing heart is sewn,
A tapestry of love, forever known.

<u>The Cartographer's Map</u>

The cartographer maps love's terrain
Ink-drawn lines, unrequited love's domain
Charting a course through passion's winding seas
A heart that journeys on, ever at ease

Ink-drawn lines, unrequited love's domain
Navigate heartache, loss, and love's refrain
A heart that journeys on, ever at ease
Finds solace in the paths that it has seized

Navigate heartache, loss, and love's refrain
Compass and parchment guide through joy and pain
Finds solace in the paths that it has seized
New lands discovered, yet the heart's not appeased

Compass and parchment guide through joy and pain
The cartographer maps love's terrain
New lands discovered, yet the heart's not appeased
Charting a course through passion's winding seas

<u>*The Clock Tower's Chime*</u>

The clock tower's chime sings a mournful song
Time marches on, my love still lingers strong

The hours pass by, a heartbeat in the night
Moments suspended, as love's tale prolongs

Each strike resounds, a bittersweet refrain
Within the chime, my yearning heart belongs

Through shadows cast, the hands of time align
Reveal a love that's patient and headstrong

In silence, waiting for the tower's call
My love, like chimes, shall never fade nor wrong

<u>*The Sailor's Hidden Currents*</u>

Our ship set sail, as friends we chose
A journey shared, on waters vast
Yet secret currents stirred below

In friendship's winds, my heart did sway
But love's uncharted seas did call
As I longed for more than friendship's bay

The moonlit waves whispered to me
Of secret dreams and hidden hearts
A love unspoken, yet so deep

An anchor weighed, yet never dropped
I sail through memories of us
One-sided love, a voyage long

Stars above, a guiding light
In search of shores, where love may dwell
My compass spins, as I hold tight

Storms may come, and waves may crest
Still, I navigate these waters
In hope, one day, my heart finds rest

But love's horizon still eludes
The sailor's heart forever lost
In unrequited seas, I cruise

<u>*Whispers of Unfulfilled Dreams*</u>

In twilight's realm, I wander through my dreams,
A realm where love and longing intertwine,
I see your face, the echoes of your laughter,
A bittersweet reminder of a love that could not be.

The moonlight casts a subtle, silvered glow,
A guiding light upon my path of yearning,
I walk the labyrinth of my heart's desire,
Seeking solace in the shadows of your memory.

I reach for you, a whisper on the wind,
But like a wisp of smoke, you slip through my fingers,
The remnants of our love, a fleeting haze,
A cruel reminder of the truth that lies awake.

In slumber's grip, I hold on to the illusion,
A world where love knows no bounds, no walls,
But as dawn breaks and morning's light emerges,
The dreamer's lament echoes through the chambers of
my soul.

I rise, a weary traveler in a world of unrequited love,
Carrying the weight of dreams unfulfilled, yet undimmed,
And as I journey through the waking world, my heart
still clings,
To whispered longings and the solace of my dreams.

The Clockmaker's Pendulum

A clockmaker's shop, where time's measured,
Each ticking hand a moment cherished,
Within the walls, a heart's love treasured,
Unrequited feelings, unbearably pleasured,
In the workshop, where gears interlace,
The clockmaker's pendulum keeps pace.

Time dances on, in steady pace,
The hands of love, meticulously measured,
In the clockmaker's craft, emotions interlace,
Unspoken dreams, silently cherished,
Through springs and cogs, a love's tale pleasured,
In each tick, a heart's love treasured.

In the workshop's air, desire treasured,
As the pendulum swings, marking life's pace,
With every chime, a memory pleasured,
Time's essence captured, framed and measured,
A love's longing, forever cherished,
In the clockmaker's hands, feelings interlace.

As the gears turn, lives interlace,
Unsaid words, a secret treasured,
In every hour, a love so cherished,
Through the passage of time, no altered pace,
In the clock's face, emotions measured,
A heart's devotion, artfully pleasured.

The clockmaker's craft, a passion pleasured,
In each creation, lives and dreams interlace,
Time's fleeting dance, artfully measured,
Within these walls, love's secrets treasured,
Ever constant, the pendulum's pace,
A love unknown, yet deeply cherished.

Unspoken wishes, secretly cherished,
In the clockmaker's heart, silently pleasured,
With every swing, the pendulum's pace,
A love's journey, gears interlace,
In the workshop's air, emotions treasured,
For love, the clockmaker's measure.

In every tick, love's weight is measured,
Each moment of longing, secretly cherished,
The clockmaker's heart, a love treasured,
In the workshop, a passion pleasured,
As the gears align and interlace,
Time's dance moves on, a steady pace.

The Florist's Arrangement

In the florist's hands, love takes form,
Petals arranged, a silent plea,
Colors tell the tale, love forlorn.

Roses red, unrequited love worn,
Amongst the blooms, a heart's decree,
In the florist's hands, love takes form.

Lilies white, purity to adorn,
Secret whispers, love's sweet decree,
Colors tell the tale, love forlorn.

Each blossom speaks, emotions transform,
A bouquet of longing, love's tapestry,
In the florist's hands, love takes form.

<u>The Clocksmith's Intricacy</u>

Gears turn, as love ticks away,
Intricate clockwork, hands intertwine,
A clocksmith's touch, time's silent play.

Unrequited love, as seconds sway,
In each movement, a hidden design,
Gears turn, as love ticks away.

Clock face, heart's desires display,
Love's persistence, a dance divine,
A clocksmith's touch, time's silent play.

Time's passage marked, love's quiet fray,
Emotions etched, each cog a sign,
Gears turn, as love ticks away.

<u>The Painter's Canvas</u>

Upon my canvas, a palette of hues
I strive to capture love's elusive muse
With tender strokes, I paint your gentle face
Yet find the colors lacking in their grace

My hand, it trembles, seeking to convey
The passion burning brightly, night and day
A masterpiece, our love that's never told
In lines and shades, a story to unfold

Alas, the canvas fails to grasp the truth
Of unrequited love that marks our youth
A portrait formed, but something still remains
A love too vast, too complex for such chains

<u>*The Sailor's Twilight*</u>

In twilight's glow, my heart sets sail,
A voyage 'cross the evening tide,
Through unrequited love, I wade.

As stars emerge, a whispered tale,
Of longing hearts, emotions chide,
In twilight's glow, my heart sets sail.

The moonlit path, a silv'ry veil,
With every wave, I hope to glide,
Through unrequited love, I wade.

To reach the shore where dreams prevail,
A place where love and loss reside,
In twilight's glow, my heart sets sail.

And as the night begins to pale,
A distant dawn, my heart will guide,
Through unrequited love, I wade.

So with a sigh, I trim the sail,
Embrace the dark, love's endless ride,
In twilight's glow, my heart sets sail,
Through unrequited love, I wade.

<u>The Architect's Blueprint</u>

An architect designs love's firmest plan
To build a love that's built to last the span
With pencil sharp and ruler steady drawn
Foundations laid, on which true love may spawn

Upon the blueprint, walls of hope arise
A shelter strong, to hold love's sweet reprise
The columns firm, of trust and faith combined
To bear the weight of love's unyielding bind

Yet as the blueprint takes its final form
The architect must face the coming storm
For love unrequited, like a gale
May shake the structure, threaten to assail

With blueprint crafted, heart and mind prepared
The architect, through love, finds strength declared
And though the storm of love may rage around
In blueprint's art, a steadfast love is found

<u>The Blacksmith's Forge</u>

The blacksmith's forge -
a heart, tempered in fire
unyielding steel

Flames dance and sway
heat and hammer, love reshaped
a stronger resolve

Red glowing embers
the fire's kiss, a new form
love's transformation

Quenched in water's depth
a bond unbroken, recast
forged anew, stronger

The Harpist's Melody

Upon my harp, a tender melody
A heartfelt song, my love's sweet elegy
Each string I pluck, a whisper soft and low
A gentle touch, to tell you how I feel

My fingers dance upon the gilded strings
Awakening notes, to which my heart clings
For in the music, hear my love's true call
A serenade, to hold you through the night

As moonlight graces every trembling chord
My melancholic tune soars heavenward
For though my love remains unclaimed, unseen
This harp's lament shall ever sing my dream

In harmony, our love's refrain shall play
And in my heart, your melody shall stay

<u>Lament of a Lonely Heart</u>

Once a man, full of love and care
For a girl with silky black hair
He loved her with all his heart
But she had someone else from the start

He tried to show her how he felt
But she never seemed to melt
Her heart belonged to another guy
Leaving him to cry and sigh

He watched as they held hands
And walked on the sandy strands
His heart was full of despair
As he watched them without a care

But still he on to hope
That one day she would see
That he was the one for her
And they could finally be

But alas, it was not meant to be
She loved another, so he had to let her be
Though his heart was broken in two
He knew he had to move on and start anew

For love is not always fair,
And sometimes it's just isnt there
But he will always cherish the memories
Of the girl he loved , but could never have, so sweetly

<u>About The Author</u>

Obscure Soul is a perceptive and enigmatic wordsmith who endeavors to make sense of life's complexities through the charm of poetry. As a profoundly introspective being, the writer grapples with numerous emotions and experiences that often remain unspoken, craving an avenue for articulation.

Motivated by a desire to convey these personal musings, Obscure Soul's verses offer a glimpse into the thoughts and feelings of someone striving to find their footing in a world that frequently feels overwhelming and lonely. Possessing a unique perspective and voice, the writer delves into themes such as affection, longing, friendship, and the silent fortitude that lies within every person.

In "Whispered Longings," Obscure Soul welcomes readers to embark on a voyage into the world of unuttered affection and the torment of unfulfilled aspirations, while also admiring the magnificence and hope that can arise even during the darkest hours. Through their stirring poetry, Obscure Soul aims to forge a connection with the audience, offering solace and understanding to those who have endured the bittersweet pain of one-sided love.

As a poet and a dreamer, Obscure Soul ceaselessly searches for novel methods to share their passion for verse and their insights into human nature. In a world that can leave us feeling disconnected, the writer's compositions serve as a reminder that we are not isolated in our struggles and that, despite the obstacles we may face, our hearts persist in beating with love, optimism, and an enduring desire to bond with others.